P8-BZU-708

The Courage of
Helen Keller

Colleen Adams

The Rosen Publishing Group's
READING ROOM
Collection

New York

Published in 2003 by The Rosen Publishing Group, Inc.
29 East 21st Street, New York, NY 10010

Copyright © 2003 by The Rosen Publishing Group, Inc.

First Library Edition 2003

All rights reserved. No part of this book may be reproduced in any form without permission in writing from the publisher, except by a reviewer.

Book Design: Haley Wilson

Photo Credits: Cover, p. 1 © Bradley Smith/Corbis; pp. 4, 6, 11, 12, 15, 19, 20–21 © Bettmann/Corbis; p. 6 (Alexander Graham Bell) © Hulton/Archive; pp. 8, 13, 17 © Corbis; p. 22 © Hulton-Deutch Collection/Corbis.

Library of Congress Cataloging-in-Publication Data

Adams, Colleen.
  The courage of Helen Keller / Colleen Adams.
      p. cm. — (The Rosen Publishing Group's reading room collection)
Includes Index.
Summary: A brief biography of Helen Keller who, with the aid and encouragement of her teacher Annie Sullivan, overcame the limitations of the deafness and blindness she suffered as a child.
  ISBN 0-8239-3710-0
  1. Keller, Helen, 1880-1968—Juvenile literature. 2. Blind-deaf women—United States—Biography—Juvenile literature. 3. Sullivan, Annie, 1866-1936—Juvenile literature. 4. Sullivan, Annie, 1866-1936. [1. Keller, Helen, 1880-1968. 2. Blind. 3. Deaf. 4. People with disabilities. 5. Women—Biography.] I. Title. II. Series.
  HV1624.K4 A33 2003
  362.4'1'092—dc21

                              2001007686

Manufactured in the United States of America

For More Information
Seeing Disabilities from a Different Perspective
http://tqjunior.thinkquest.org/5852/homepg.htm

American Foundation for the Blind
http://www.afb.org/info_documents.asp?kitid=9&collectionid=1

Contents

4

Helen's Sickness

Helen Keller was born in a little town in Alabama on June 27, 1880. Shortly before her second birthday, she became very sick with a high **fever**. The fever made her lose her sight and hearing. Helen learned how to recognize people by touching their faces or clothes. She made up more than sixty **gestures** to **communicate** with people around her.

When Helen was a child, she liked to play with her dog, Lioness.

Alexander Graham Bell

6

Help for Helen

Helen faced many struggles trying to communicate with others. This often made her angry. Sometimes she screamed, cried, and threw things. Her parents could not always calm her. They began to look for a teacher who could help her.

Helen's father asked Dr. Alexander Graham Bell to help them. Dr. Bell was the famous inventor of the telephone and a teacher of the **deaf**. Bell said that a special school for the blind in Boston may have a teacher who could work with Helen.

Helen's parents wanted her to learn how to communicate with others. They also wanted her to learn how to read and write.

Anne Sullivan

The Perkins School for the Blind sent a teacher named Anne Sullivan to live with the Kellers shortly before Helen's seventh birthday. Anne taught Helen that it was not right to scream and throw things. Soon Helen learned to trust Anne and follow her rules. With Anne's help, Helen quickly learned a method of **sign language** called finger spelling. This is a way of spelling by using your fingers to shape letters onto the open hand of a deaf person so they can feel them.

▼ Helen learned to read lips by feeling the movements of Anne's mouth as she talked.

At first, Helen did not understand finger spelling. Anne continued to use it, hoping Helen would finally understand that the signs spelled words that named things. One day when they were out walking, Anne and Helen passed a well. Anne pumped water from the well over Helen's hand while she spelled W-A-T-E-R in Helen's other hand. Anne kept doing this until Helen understood that she was spelling the word "water."

Helen suddenly understood that Anne was showing her how to communicate with finger spelling, and a whole new world opened up to her.

In just six months, Helen learned over 600 words in sign language. By the time she was eight years old, she could print words and sentences using a special board with **grooves** in it. Anne also taught Helen to read **braille** (BRAYL), a system of raised dots that stand for different letters of the alphabet. A person reads the dots by touching them with their fingers.

When Helen was an adult, she often gave speeches.
In the photo above, Helen is giving a speech on the braille
alphabet and the man who created it, Louis Braille.

13

More to Learn

Anne wanted Helen to learn more. She took her to the Perkins School for the Blind in 1888. Helen learned to understand different languages like German and French. With the help of her speech teacher, Sarah Fuller, Helen learned to speak for the first time when she was nine. Helen and Anne traveled all over the country and met many famous people. Helen became close friends with Alexander Graham Bell and visited him often as she grew up. They remained lifelong friends.

Helen later wrote about her special friendship with ▼
Alexander Graham Bell in a book about her life.

15

A Dream Comes True

To prepare for college, Helen decided to go to the Cambridge School for Young Ladies in Boston. Many people didn't think she would be able to keep up with the other students. Helen worked very hard to prove that she could. She studied French, history, and math. Anne went to all of Helen's classes and taught her the lessons in sign language.

Helen became popular at school but did not have much extra time to do fun things with her friends. She spent most of her time studying and writing.

17

In 1900, Helen entered Radcliffe College in Cambridge, Massachusetts. Helen knew she would have to work harder than anyone else to keep up with her studies. She also found time to write her first book, *The Story of My Life.* Helen wanted to share her feelings and tell her story to other people. *The Story of My Life* was published in 1903. It was the first of twelve books Helen wrote during her lifetime. Helen **graduated** from college with honors in 1904.

Helen became the first deaf and blind person to graduate from college.

19

Helping Others

After college, Helen wanted to help other people. She traveled around the country with Anne and gave speeches about the rights of **disabled** people, women's rights, and **civil rights**. Many people came to hear her. It took **courage** for Helen to speak to people about her life and beliefs.

In 1916, Helen and Anne met a woman named Polly Thompson. Polly worked for Helen as a housekeeper and became a lifelong friend.

▼ Polly, Helen, and Anne met many people as they traveled to France, England, Ireland, Japan, and many other countries throughout the world.

Helen's Gift

Anne died in 1936 after spending forty-eight years as a teacher and friend to Helen. Helen continued to travel and help disabled people throughout the world with Polly at her side. She received many honors for helping disabled people and **inspired** many people with her love of life. Helen died in 1968 just before her eighty-eighth birthday.

Glossary

braille   A system of writing for blind people. Groups of raised dots stand for letters and numbers, and are read by touching them.

civil rights   A person's rights as a citizen of the United States of America.

communicate   To make something known.

courage   The ability to face trouble instead of running away from it.

deaf   Unable to hear.

disabled   To have lost the power to do something, such as seeing, hearing, or walking, because of illness.

fever   When a person's body is warmer than normal.

gesture   A movement of the hands, arms, or any part of the body.

graduate   To finish the course of studies of a school or college.

groove   A long, narrow line cut into a piece of wood.

inspire   To cause someone else to have a good thought or good feeling.

sign language   A language in which motions of the fingers, hands, and arms stand for letters, words, and ideas.

Index